The **SCIENCE BOOK** for **GIRLS**

and Other Intelligent Beings

Written by Valerie Wyatt
Illustrated by Pat Cupples

KIDS CAN PRESS

To the women of science — past, present
and, especially, future

First U.S. edition 1997

Kids Can Press acknowledges the financial support of the Ontario Arts Council, the Canada Council
for the Arts and the Government of Canada, through the BPIDP, for our publishing activity.

Published in Canada by
Kids Can Press Ltd.
29 Birch Avenue
Toronto, ON M4V 1E2

Published in the U.S. by
Kids Can Press Ltd.
2250 Military Road
Tonawanda, NY 14150

Edited by Charis Wahl
Interior designed by Nancy Ruth Jackson
Cover designed by Karen Powers
Cover photos by Ray Boudreau

Printed in Hong Kong by Wing King Tong Company Limited

This book is limp sewn with a drawn-on cover.

CMC 93 0 9 8

Canadian Cataloguing in Publication Data

Wyatt, Valerie
The science book for girls and other intelligent beings

Includes index.
ISBN 1-55074-113-6

1. Science — Juvenile literature. 2. Women scientists
— Biography — Juvenile literature. 3. Scientific
recreations — Juvenile literature. I. Cupples,
Patricia. II. Title.

Q163.W93 1993   j500   C93-094020-2

Kids Can Press is a Nelvana company

Contents

Chapter 1: Everyday Science 7

Experiment with the amazing scientific events of an ordinary day:

food chemistry (10); rain (12); microorganisms (14); ink
chromatography (16); digestion (18); sandwich and map math (22);
why things tarnish and spin (24); more food chemistry (26); collecting
and presenting data (28); TV viewing (30); and the science of soap,
toothpaste and stars (32).

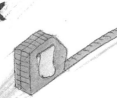

Chapter 2: Be a Scientist 34

**Try on a few sciences and see which one suits you best.
Maybe you'll be:**

an archaeologist (36), a geologist (40), a physicist (42), a zoologist
(45), a botanist (48), a chemist (50), a meteorologist (52), an
environmental scientist (54), a geneticist (56) or an astronomer (58).

Chapter 3: Flex Your Science Muscles 60

Warm up your brain with these visual puzzles and brain benders.

Acknowledgments

All books are group efforts, this one more than most. It began several years ago with a phone call to Mary Vickers, the chair of the Girls in Science committee of the Society for Canadian Women in Science and Technology (SCWIST), and has involved literally hundreds of people since then.

Mary Vickers was there from start to finish — setting up meetings, coming up with ideas and arranging for hundreds of girls in Canada and the United States to test material. She is the real fairy godmother behind this project. Other members of SCWIST were also extremely helpful. Thank you to Girl Science committee members Marion Adair, Sarah Groves, Betty Howard, Penny Le Couteur, Eileen Mackay, Elspeth Russell and Wendy Scholefield for their support and encouragement, and to SCWIST members Fran Aitkens and Jackie Gill for their editorial help.

Testing of material for the book was undertaken by the following with the help of financial support from the Government of Canada, Science Culture Canada program: Beverly LeMoine, MacDonald Drive Elementary School, St. John's, NF; Lawrence Delbridge, N.S. Department of Education; Margaret Joyce, Eliot River School, Cornwall, PEI; Darlene Whitehouse, N.B. Department of Education; Debbie Nicoll-Griffith, Whiteside Taylor Daycare, Baie D'Urfé, PQ; Bonnie Taylor Gillings, Colonel John Butler School, Niagara-on-the-Lake, ON; Miriam Maltz and Paulette Migie, Ramah School, Winnipeg, MB; Glenis Joyce, University of Saskatchewan; Lois Baillie, Moose Jaw, SK; Patricia Campbell, Sifton School, Edmonton, AB; Margaret Ann Armour, University of Alberta; Frances Bates, Richmond, BC; Kathleen Murison, Crofton House, Vancouver, BC; Eileen Mackay, Crofton House, Vancouver, BC; Glenda Johnstone, Surrey, BC; Ardy Smith, Yukon Department of Education; Pat Duncan, Whitehorse, YT; Judy Foster, Elizabeth MacKenzie School, Rae-Edzo, NT; Terrence Bradley, J.H. Sissons School, Yellowknife, NT; Mary Meeker, Girl Smart, Walla Walla, WA. Thank you all.

Special thanks to the testers — more than 400 girls aged 8 to 12 in schools, science clubs and other groups. Wish there were room to name you all. And to Fiona Downie, Hilary Morrice, Kate Tucker and Rhianydd Bellis, who tested experiments on their own — and, in Rhianydd's case, donated hair for the hygrometer on page 13.

A number of scientists helped check the accuracy of statements in the book. (Any inaccuracies that have crept in are solely my responsibility.) In particular, I would like to thank: Kelly Akers, University of Toronto; C. Duitschaever, University of Guelph; Ross James, Royal Ontario Museum; Clifford Leznoff, York University; Gilbert MacArthur and Nick Massey, B.C. Ministry of Energy, Mines and Petroleum Resources; Dave Malloch, University of Toronto; Ian McGregor, Royal Ontario Museum; Hooley McLaughlin, Ontario Science Centre; G. Monette, York University; Marty Morrice; Patricia Stewart, University of Toronto; Patrick Tevlin, Ontario Science Centre. Thanks especially to Katherine Farris for her painstaking and cheerful checking and to Chris McGowan of the Royal Ontario Museum, who generously read the entire manuscript and made many excellent suggestions.

The people at Kids Can Press were, as always, a pleasure to work with and a source of many creative solutions. Thank you to Michael Solomon for his initial work on the design and to Blair and Brooke Kerrigan for their timely contribution to the title and cover design; to Nancy Ruth Jackson, designer, and Pat Cupples, illustrator, whose talents individually and combined are truly awesome; to Lori Burwash, for her enthusiasm, patience and care as a copy editor and production editor; to Charis Wahl, my editor, for putting words in Nora's mouth and vastly improving the rest of the words in the book; to Valerie Hussey and Ricky Englander, for their support throughout this project.

Finally, I would like to thank my husband, Larry MacDonald, for being a combination sounding board, idea generator and cheering section — and for putting up with the mess in the kitchen as I tested experiments.

CHAPTER 1
EVERYDAY SCIENCE

What is that awful ringing in your ears? You pull a pillow over your head, but the noise doesn't go away. You have a terrible thought: that ringing is your alarm clock. How can it be morning? You just went to bed. You open one eye. Argh! Sunshine.

You stick one hand out from under the covers and feel around under the bed. Fur and a growl. It's Spike, the cat. Then you touch — oh yuck! — a very mushy banana. Finally — yes! You're in luck. You hook one finger through the belt loop of your jeans, drag them under the covers and pull them on. Half dressed and you're still in bed. Not bad.

Now what to wear on top? Your shark T-shirt. You try the floor again, but all you get is another growl from Spike. This calls for drastic action. You'll have to get up.

You stumble around the bedroom, looking for your T-shirt and trying to forget what your mother said last night: "No wonder you can never find anything. Your room looks like a pigpen. No, that's not fair — pigs are cleaner."

You haven't time to clean up. You've got to find that T-shirt soon or else be late for school. You lift a bathrobe off the floor. Nothing underneath. There's no sense looking in the closet — few of your clothes get that far. As you flop down on the bed, you hear a high-pitched, muffled squeal. You jump up and peel back a mound of covers.

There, sprawled on the sheet, is a very small person with a very big magnifying glass. She's wearing a white coat and in-line skates so small they would fit your Barbie doll.

"You almost flattened me," she says, as she picks herself up.

"Who are you?" you ask.

"I'm a Natural Observation Research Activator." She grins at your shocked look. "You might be more familiar with my old name — fairy godmother."

"A fairy godmother?" you stutter. "What are you doing here?"

"Looking for dust mites," she replies.

"In my bed?"

"You bet. They live off the tiny flakes of skin you shed. And they never go hungry."

"That's disgusting." This is getting very weird. A tiny person is searching your bed for bugs that eat cast-off skin. Your brain feels like a computer about to crash … and then it comes up with an idea.

"Hey, if you're a fairy godmother — "

"Natural Observation Research Activator," she interrupts. "Just call me Nora."

"Whatever. Can you find my T-shirt with the shark on the front?" Instantly, the long-lost T-shirt emerges from a beach bag and floats before your eyes.

"Old-fashioned magic," says Nora. "Frogs into princes. Petrified forests. Once-upon-a-time hoo-ha. Lost interest in it years ago. Now science," she says, peering at you through her magnifying glass, "that's something else. Amazing scientific events are happening all around you every minute of the day."

"No way!"

"I'll prove it to you. Let's start with your breakfast." She flies out the door before you have time to say "shazam."

You pull on your shark T-shirt and follow. It's going to be an interesting day.

This dust mite (magnified hundreds of times) never goes hungry. It feeds on the 0.5 kg (1 pound) of skin flakes you shed every year.

Chemistry for breakfast?

You pop a piece of bread in the toaster, slice an apple over your cereal and pour on the milk.

"No science so far," you say to Nora.

"Oh yeah?" she replies. "Take a look. Your soft white bread is tanned and crispy, the apple slices are going brown, and your cereal is soggy. Your breakfast is chemistry in action."

A TOAST TEST

What happens to bread as it toasts? Try some science and see. Before you get started, spread newspaper over your work area so you don't make a major mess. Iodine stains.

You'll need:

a slice of white bread, cut in half
a teaspoon
iodine (the kind you put on cuts and scrapes)
a glass half filled with water
a saucer

1. Toast one half of the bread until the cut edge is a very dark brown.

2. Mix a spoonful of iodine in the water, then pour some of the iodine-water mixture into the saucer.

3. Dip the cut edge of the **untoasted** bread into the saucer of iodine and water. What happens? The iodine on the bread turns purple. It's saying, "There's lots of starch in this bread."

4. Dip the cut edge of the **toasted** bread into the saucer of iodine and water. What happens to the iodine? That's right — nothing. Now it's saying, "No starch here."

The heat of toasting has changed the starch into a kind of sugar. Your body does the same thing: it turns starchy foods into sugar. Then it uses the sugar for energy.

Does cooking always turn starch into sugar?

Cook other starchy foods — try potatoes or pasta — and give them the iodine test.

SNAP, CRACKLE AND SOG

Milk has a bad influence on breakfast cereal. Add milk to even the crunchiest cereal and, in minutes, the cereal sogs. Do some cereals get soggy faster than others? See for yourself.

You'll need:

3 kinds of breakfast cereals. (Try O-shaped cereals, flakes and puffs. Use all sugar-coated or all unsugared cereals. Don't mix the two types.)

3 identical small bowls

150 mL (³/4 cup) of milk

a measuring cup

a watch or clock

1. Pour 50 mL (¹/4 cup) of each kind of cereal into separate bowls.

2. Pour 50 mL (¹/4 cup) of milk into each bowl.

3. After one minute, taste the cereals. Do any seem soggy?

4. Wait a minute, then taste the cereals again. Keep tasting until all the cereals are soggy. Keep a record of which cereal sogs first, second and third. Why do you think certain cereals get soggy sooner than others?

If you stuck a piece of cereal under a microscope, you'd see that it was filled with tiny air spaces that look like little empty tubes. Liquid travels up these tubes, making the cereal seem waterlogged. The same thing happens in bath towels, paper towels and sponges. It's called capillary action.

Bad apples

How long does it take an apple slice to go brown? Time it. Do thin slices go brown faster than thick ones? The brown color is caused when oxygen in the air comes into contact with chemicals in the apple. The brown stuff acts as a shield, protecting the rest of the apple from the oxygen so the whole apple doesn't go brown.

A wet walk to school

You invite Nora to go to school with you. Maybe she'll work some old-fashioned magic on your unfinished homework.

Just as you head out the door, the rain starts. It's five blocks to school. "Hmmmmm. Should I run or walk?"

"Scientists have studied that question," says Nora, who is wearing a raincoat that looks suspiciously like your Barbie doll's. "If you run, you'll be out in the rain for a shorter time."

You take a deep breath, ready to make a dash for it.

"But you'll also run into drops and get wet from them as well. You need to figure out whether more raindrops will hit you running or walking."

Math to keep you dry

Suppose it takes ten minutes to walk to school and five minutes to run there. And suppose 200 raindrops a minute fall on you when you walk. Only 150 raindrops a minute fall on you when you run, but you run into another 75 raindrops a minute. Will you stay drier running or walking? Answer on page 78.

12

RAIN OR SHINE?

This rain predictor will help you decide when you need your umbrella. It's called a hair hygrometer. Why? Read on ...

You'll need:

scissors
a straw
sticky tape
a long blond hair, washed
   with soap, rinsed and dried
a pin
a shoebox

1. Cut a piece of straw about 10 cm (4 inches) long. Cut one end on an angle. Wrap that end with tape.

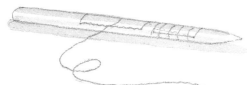

2. Tape one end of the hair to the straw as shown.

3. Pin the straw 7 cm (3 inches) up from the bottom of the box.

4. Stretch the hair up the box. When the straw is pointed slightly up and the hair is taut, tape the free end of the hair to the box.

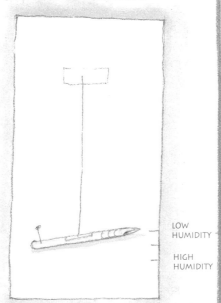

LOW HUMIDITY

HIGH HUMIDITY

5. What happens when there is lots of moisture in the air? Put the box in the bathroom when you're taking a bath or shower. Where does the straw point? Label that place "high humidity."

6. Take the box out of the bathroom and use a hair dryer to dry the hair. Where does the straw point? Label that place "low humidity."

7. Check the box daily. If the straw points to "high humidity," better take your umbrella. The hair is stretching because there's lots of humidity in the air, so it might rain.

Umbrella inventors

In 1986 a five-year-old Indiana girl named Katie Harding had a brilliant idea. Her brother kept coming home with wet feet from accidentally walking through puddles on dark rainy days. What he needed was a way to see the puddles before he stepped in them. So Katie attached a flashlight to an umbrella and presto — no more wet feet.

Katie was improving on a 3500-year-old invention. The first umbrellas were sunshades. The women of ancient Rome turned them into rain protectors by coating them with oil.

The invisible inhabitants of room 22

You peel off your wet raincoat and look around the classroom. "For once, I'm here first."

"Uh uh," says Nora, shaking her head. "This place is full."

There is definitely no one else in the room.

Nora holds up a pin. "There are about ten thousand of them on the head of this pin. Millions are cruising around your desk and swimming through the air you're breathing."

Is Nora into horror movies? You look around nervously.

"Microorganisms," Nora announces. "Micro means small."

"Good thing."

"Want to see some for yourself?"

SEEING THE INVISIBLE

Microorganisms are so small you would need a microscope to see them. But you can collect plant-like microorganisms called mold and get a good look at them.

You'll need:

a slice of white bread cut in quarters
water
paper towels
4 small clear plastic bags with twist ties (sandwich bags work well)
4 labels
a pen

1. Slightly dampen your bread quarters by sprinkling water on them.

2. Collect some dust and sprinkle it on one bread quarter. (If it's difficult to pick up the dust, just wipe the bread quarter over a dusty area.) Place the bread dust-side up on a damp paper towel.

3. Put the bread and paper towel in a plastic bag. Blow in some air and close the bag with a twist tie. Label the bag with where the dust came from.

4. Collect dust from a different place on each bread quarter. Include a bit of dust from a vacuum cleaner, if you wish. Bag the dust samples as you did in step 3 and label where each came from.

5. Put your bags in a warm, dark place. Check them every day, but do not open the bags. Do white patches appear on the bread? Later, are there black dots? These are the beginnings of bread-mold colonies. Mold spores (which are too small to see) are a bit like seeds. They hitchhike on dust particles. If they are lucky, they land on some nice moist food and grow.

When you've finished your experiment, throw out your bagged molds, without opening the bags.

Which locations produced the most mold? Is bread the only good mold home? Try the same experiment using different foods to feed your mold.

The good, the bad and the ugly

There are millions of kinds of microorganisms.
• The vinegar on your salad was wine until microorganisms went to work on it. Microorganisms also turn milk into yogurt and cheese.
• Yeast microorganisms "burp" carbon dioxide gas, which makes the holes in your bread.
• Algae (the green slimy stuff) in fish tanks, lakes and ponds is actually millions of tiny microorganisms.
• The viruses that cause mumps and chickenpox are microorganisms. Some viruses, such as the ones that give you the flu, can be spread by sneezing.
• A variety of microorganisms help to break down garbage and turn it into soil. That's what happens when you compost.

You call it doodling, I call it science

You are supposed to be looking for science fair ideas; instead, you're trying out your new black felt pen. You've just added arms and legs to a flower when Nora lands on your shoulder.

"Nice colors," she says.

You look at your drawing and then at her. "You must be seeing things — or using your magic powers."

"Nope ... just some colorful science."

AMAZE-INK!

Is black felt-pen ink really black? Try this and see.

You'll need:

scissors
a white coffee filter
sticky tape
a pencil
a black felt pen that is "water-soluble"
    or "washable." (Look for these words
    on the side of the pen.)
a glass
water

1. Cut a strip of filter paper about 2.5 cm (1 inch) wide and 12 cm (4½ inches) long.

2. Tape one edge of the strip to the pencil. Near the other edge, put a scribble of black felt-pen ink. The scribble should be about 2 cm (¾ inch) up from the bottom of the paper.

3. Rest the pencil across the rim of the glass so that the filter paper hangs without touching the sides or bottom of the glass.

4. Pour water into the glass until the bottom of the paper—but not the part with the ink on it — is dangling in the water. (Be careful not to pour the water directly onto the paper.) The water will travel up tiny tubes in the paper by capillary action.

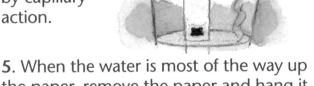

5. When the water is most of the way up the paper, remove the paper and hang it somewhere to dry.

Was the black ink more colorful than you expected? Black ink is a mixture of pigments. Water acts as a solvent (dissolver) and separates the pigments. How?

Some pigments stick to the filter paper more than others. One by one, the pigments lose hold and are carried up the paper by the water. (Think of a bunch of kids in a wave pool, all holding on to the same air mattress. They look like one big mass of arms and legs, but one by one they let go and get carried along by the waves.) The process of separating colored mixtures is called chromatography.

The amaze-ink science fair project

Does searching for a science fair idea make your knees knock, your hands tremble and your stomach churn? Relax. Here's an amaze-ink idea.

Will water separate all inks, or does it just work with water-soluble markers? Will solvents other than water work? Test a variety of pen inks with a variety of liquids, such as vinegar, lemon juice and rubbing alcohol. Make a chart to keep track of your results.

PEN	WATER	VINEGAR	LEMON JUICE	RUBBING ALCOHOL
WATER-SOLUBLE FELT PEN				
OTHER FELT PEN				
BALL-POINT PEN				
FOUNTAIN PEN				

Trying using a wet Smartie or M & M candy as your ink. Can you separate the colors?

Lunch!

Ten minutes to go and the seconds are crawling by. Suddenly, a terrible rumbling, grumbling roar starts in your stomach.

"Borborygmus," whispers Nora.

She must have you mixed up with someone else. "Borborwho?"

"That rumbling in your stomach is called borborygmus. Embarrassing, isn't it?"

Your red face says it all.

"It happens when your stomach tries to mix food that isn't there. Air gets tumbled around instead." Nora does a triple back flip to demonstrate. "That's what makes the growling sound. And when the air pushes up against the walls of your stomach, you feel pain — hunger pangs. Poor you."

The bell rings. You grab your lunch bag and head for the lunch room. Fifteen minutes later, there's nothing but a few crumbs left.

"You haven't finished your lunch," says Nora.

"Sure I have." You point to the empty bag.

"You may have swallowed it, but your lunch is now on a journey that makes a roller-coaster ride look like a Sunday snooze."

Your lunch's perilous journey

Inside you is a food processor that's almost 7 m (21 feet) long. Your digestive tract mushes and smushes your food into tiny bits so the nutrients can be absorbed by your body and used as fuel. Here's what happens to your lunch.

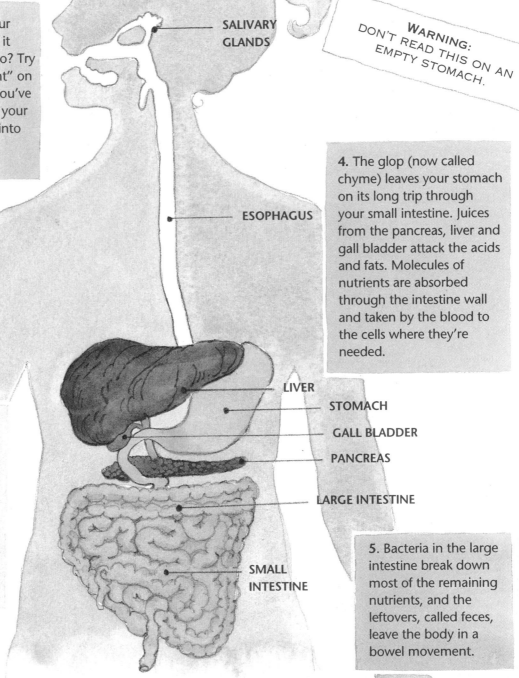

1. You start breaking down your food by chewing it and mixing it with saliva. (What does saliva do? Try "A Mouth-watering Experiment" on page 21 and find out.) When you've mashed up the mouthful a bit, your tongue shoves the food down into your esophagus (throat).

2. Your bite of food is now called a bolus because it's ball-shaped. (Bolus is Latin for "ball.") Muscles in your esophagus force the bolus down into your stomach. This muscle action, called peristalsis, is a bit like squeezing toothpaste out of a tube.

3. Stomach juices — including hydrochloric acid, which is so powerful it can strip paint off a car — break down the bolus. Peristalsis continues, mixing the food and juices non-stop until the food is like porridge. At any time, there's about 1 L (1 quart) of food in your stomach — enough to fill a milk carton.

4. The glop (now called chyme) leaves your stomach on its long trip through your small intestine. Juices from the pancreas, liver and gall bladder attack the acids and fats. Molecules of nutrients are absorbed through the intestine wall and taken by the blood to the cells where they're needed.

5. Bacteria in the large intestine break down most of the remaining nutrients, and the leftovers, called feces, leave the body in a bowel movement.

WARNING: DON'T READ THIS ON AN EMPTY STOMACH.

SALIVARY GLANDS

ESOPHAGUS

LIVER

STOMACH

GALL BLADDER

PANCREAS

LARGE INTESTINE

SMALL INTESTINE

SWALLOW THIS

When someone asks why you're standing on your head eating a banana, tell her you are doing a science experiment.

You'll need:

a soft cushion
a friend
a small, bite-sized piece of banana, peeled

1. Stand on your head, with your head on the cushion. (This is the part you need the friend for.)

2. While you are doing your headstand, chew and swallow the piece of banana — very carefully. Try not to giggle while you do this.

The muscles of your esophagus are so powerful that they force food into your stomach even when you're upside down.

CORNY BUT INTERESTING

Some foods are so tough that even your digestive tract can't mush them. Corn is a real toughy. Because some kernels stay whole all the way down, you can use them to time how long digestion takes.

You'll need:

corn on the cob or frozen or canned corn

1. Eat as much corn as you'd usually eat at a meal. Make a note of the day and time.

2. Next time you have a bowel movement, check to see if there are corn kernels in your feces. Keep checking each bowel movement until you see some corn kernels. Note the time and calculate how long it took the corn to travel through your system.

A MOUTH-WATERING EXPERIMENT

Ever notice how your mouth waters when you're about to eat something great? There's a reason for all that saliva. Try this to find out why.

You'll need:

masking tape and a pen
4 small dishes
iodine (the kind you put on cuts and scrapes)
2 soda crackers
a watch or timer

1. With the pen and masking tape, make labels for the four dishes: "unchewed," "30 seconds," "5 minutes," "10 minutes."

2. Put a drop of iodine on one of the crackers and put it in the dish labeled "unchewed." Does the iodine turn dark blue? That means the cracker is full of starch. Iodine is a starch detector.

3. Chew the other cracker and put a third of it in each of the other dishes. Put a drop of iodine on the cracker in the "30 seconds" dish. Does the iodine change color?

4. Wait five minutes. Put a drop of iodine on the cracker in the "5 minutes" dish. What happens to the iodine this time?

5. Wait another five minutes. Test the cracker in the "10 minutes" dish.

Which of the crackers had the most starch? As your saliva got to work on the cracker, it broke down the starch and turned it into a form of sugar that your body could use. Did time make a difference?

You will swallow 36 000 kg (40 tons) of food during your lifetime. Urpbay!

Real-life math

If you hurry, you might be able to finish your homework before the bell.

"Know anything about math?" you ask Nora innocently.

"You bet. Scientists use math all the time. So do Natural Observation Research Activators."

"Great. You can help." You read Nora the first question. "You and your four sisters are shipwrecked on a desert island. You have nine sandwiches. If you shared the sandwiches equally, how many would each of you get?"

What kind of dweeb thinks up math questions? you wonder. Fat chance you'll ever be on a desert island with four sisters and nine sandwiches. Suddenly you are whirling around, and everything is a blur. When you stop whirling, you are on a beach. There's a palm tree, sand, water — hey, cool.

Then you notice a kicking, punching, yelling mass of arms and legs. Welcome to your nightmare. Four little girls.

"NORA!" you shout.

"Haven't lost my touch, have I?" She is beaming with pride. "Thought you might like some real-life math." Then she disappears.

Oh great. You are stranded on a desert island with four brats yelling, "That's my sandwich!" "No, it's mine." "I want it!" You'd better get calculating.

The great sandwich divide

You pry apart the little monsters and give each a sandwich. You eat a sandwich yourself. The girls are screaming for more. You cut the rest of the sandwiches in half. You eat one of the halves and give each of your "sisters" a half. There are still some sandwiches left, so you cut them in half again. Now you've got a bunch of quarter-sandwiches. You give each girl a quarter. You eat a quarter yourself and secretly slip another quarter into your pocket. Not counting the sandwich in your pocket, how many quarters are left? Answer on page 78.

Mapping the distance

Down the beach you can hear the sound of four little girls stomping up and down, chanting "Trea-sure, trea-sure." They have found a map. Sure enough, it shows a trunk filled with coins and jewels. And – wait a minute – it shows a town on a nearby island. If you can get there, maybe you can find someone to take the girls. That'd be even better than buried treasure.

But, oh-oh! There's also a shark. And the only way you can get anywhere is by swimming! More real-life math. Would you be better off swimming to the treasure island and then to the town? Or should you swim directly to the town? Which of those two routes is shorter? (After all, shorter means less time with the shark.)

Measure the distances to find out. Use the red Xs as your measuring points. Oh ... and good luck!

SCALE

0   1   2

KILOMETRES

Science at work (and play)

There's a note on the fridge when you get home. The handwriting looks as if a three-year-old wrote it holding a blunt crayon between his toes.

HEY SIS, MIKEY HAS LENT ME HIS IN-LINE SKATES. THREE BUCKS IF YOU DO MY CHORES BEFORE THE PARENTS GET HOME. AND HEY—HAVE FUN!

YOUR FAVE BROTHER,

JASON

Typical. Oh well, three dollars is three dollars. You reach into the chore bowl hoping to pick an easy one, like watering the plants. No such luck: "Bathe the dog." You look at the dog. The dog looks at you. You put the slip back in the bowl. The dog wags her tail.

You pick another slip: "Polish the silver."

"Magic would really come in handy here," you say casually. But does Nora get the hint?

HI HO, SILVER!

Arghh! Those knives and forks look as if they haven't been polished since the dinosaurs died. Yuck! Slop on the polish. Wait till it dries. Rub, rub, rub.

"You don't need magic," Nora says. "Just science."

You'll need:

a frying pan without a non-stick coating
aluminum foil
water
baking soda
salt
some tarnished knives, forks and spoons
tongs

1. Line the bottom and sides of the pan with aluminum foil.

2. Pour in 1 L (4 cups) of water and 5 mL (1 teaspoon) each of baking soda and salt. Stir.

3. Put one layer of silverware in the pan. Each piece must touch the aluminum foil. (It's okay if the pieces touch one another.) If the water doesn't cover the silverware, add more till it does.

4. Ask an adult to help you put the pan on the stove and gently boil the water. What happens to the tarnish? Remove the silverware from the water with the tongs. Let the pieces cool. Then shine them up with a soft rag.

Tarnish is silver sulphide. It forms when sulphur in foods or in the air attacks the silverware. When you put the tarnished silverware into the frying pan, there's an electro-chemical reaction. This turns the silver from dull silver sulphide back into the shiny form of silver.

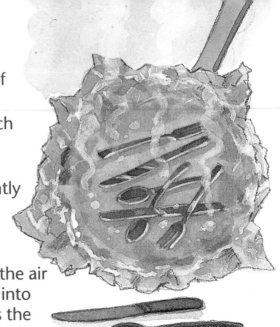

FRISBEE FUN

The dog appears with a Frisbee in her mouth just as you lift that last fork out of the pan.

"Ever wonder how something without wings can fly?" asks Nora, perching on the Frisbee.

"You don't have wings and you can fly."

"I'm special," she says, with a loop and a spin. "Frisbees are scientific. Here's how they fly."

You'll need:

a piece of string about 1 m (3 feet) long
a long-playing record that
    no one wants
a pencil

1. Thread the string through the hole in the record. Hold it in place with the pencil as shown.

2. Hold the free end of the string and swing the record from side to side. Having trouble? Spin the record before you swing it.

Spinning makes the record stable: a Frisbee spins about 300 times a minute. But that's not all that keeps it airborne. Its front edge tilts up slightly as it cuts through the air. This creates "lift," the same force that allows airplane wings to keep planes flying.

25

Dinner is served ... scientifically

It's your turn to cook dinner. You flip through a cookbook. The pictures look yummy, but when you look at the recipes ... whew! Long lists of ingredients. Pages of instructions. Everything looks too hard. Where is Nora when you need her? Maybe she could work some old-fashioned magic on this meal.

"I'm here ... but forget the magic." You are about to start begging when she saves the day. "I'll show you how to put science to work to cook your dinner. How does String Soup sound, followed by Different Dogs and Hot Snowballs?"

You haven't a clue what she's talking about, but you'd eat grape-noodle soup and chicken-fat-ripple ice cream as long as you didn't have to make them.

STRING SOUP

The science in this soup is so surprising, it looks like magic.

You'll need:

a can of chicken broth
a pot
water
a raw egg
a measuring cup or small bowl
a fork

1. Empty the broth into the pot and add water according to the instructions on the can. Put the pot on the stove and cook at high heat. Ask an adult to help you when you're using the stove.

2. While you're waiting for the soup to heat up, break the egg into a measuring cup and beat it with a fork.

3. When the soup is boiling, turn the heat down to low and wait for the bubbles to subside. Then trickle the egg slowly into the soup in a thin stream. Use the fork to swirl the soup gently as you pour. Notice anything strange?

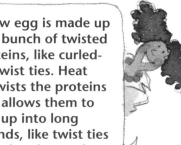

A raw egg is made up of a bunch of twisted proteins, like curled-up twist ties. Heat untwists the proteins and allows them to join up into long strands, like twist ties joined end to end.

DIFFERENT DOGS

Do wieners change depending on how you cook them? See for yourself, then see why on page 78.

Boil 'em: Cook a wiener in a pot of water at a low boil. Watch the wiener as it cooks. Does it roll over? How often? Time it and see. Why does it keep rolling as it cooks?

Fry 'em: Put a wiener in a non-stick fry pan and turn the heat to medium. What happens to the wiener. Why?

Nuke 'em: Put a wiener in a microwave oven and turn it on to high for 30 seconds. What happens? Why?

Why do hot-dog buns get mushy in a microwave? See page 78.

HOT SNOWBALLS

How can a snowball be hot? Try this and see.

You'll need:

2 egg whites (Ask an adult to help you separate the whites from the yolks. It's important that no yolk gets into the whites.)

a clean, dry glass or ceramic bowl

an eggbeater

6 flat cookies without any icing or filling

a cookie sheet

a spoon

some ice cream

1. Turn on the oven to 120°C (250°F).

2. Put the egg whites in the bowl and beat them. Stop the eggbeater from time to time. Use it to lift some egg whites. When they stand in stiff, moist peaks, they're ready.

3. Put the cookies on the cookie sheet. Spoon a small mound of ice cream onto the middle of each cookie. Make sure bare cookie shows all around the ice cream.

4. Spoon egg white over each ice-cream mound. The egg white should completely cover the ice cream and the bare cookie around it. Make sure there's no ice cream showing.

5. Put the snowballs in the oven for four minutes, or until the egg white turns light brown. Take the cookie sheet out and eat your cooked snowballs. Ask an adult to help you use the oven.

The foamy egg white acts as insulation. The air bubbles you whipped into it stop the heat from getting through to the ice cream.

27

Hello! Hello?

You are on the phone with your friend Jasmine when Jason slips you a note.

GET OFF THE PHONE!

You would ignore it, but Jason has your diary in one hand and the key in the other. He means business — your business.

You hang up and growl at him. "Pest."

"Motor mouth."

"Ding-a-ling."

"You yap on the phone more than the rest of the family put together," says Jason.

"That's because no one wants to talk to you," you snarl, grabbing both diary and key.

WHO'S ON THE PHONE?

When Nora shows up, you are plotting your revenge. "Jason uses the phone just as much as I do, and I'm going to prove it."

"How?"

"I'm going to keep track of all phone calls in and out of this house for five days."

You'll need:

a watch or clock
a pencil and paper
2 kinds of stickers

1. Do your phone survey on five nights when everyone in the family is home. It doesn't have to be five nights in a row — any five nights will do. Write down all incoming and outgoing phone calls during the same four-hour period each night. Record the number of calls and the length of each call on a chart.

2. Total the "calls" and "time" for each person. Now you've got the evidence (scientists call these numbers "data") to test your idea (or "hypothesis") that Jason uses the phone just as much as you do.

3. To be really scientific, present your data on a graph. Start with a "call" graph. Use one sticker for each call. Your final graph might look like the one on the left.

4. Now graph "time." Let each sticker represent the same amount of time, say five minutes. See the graph on the right.

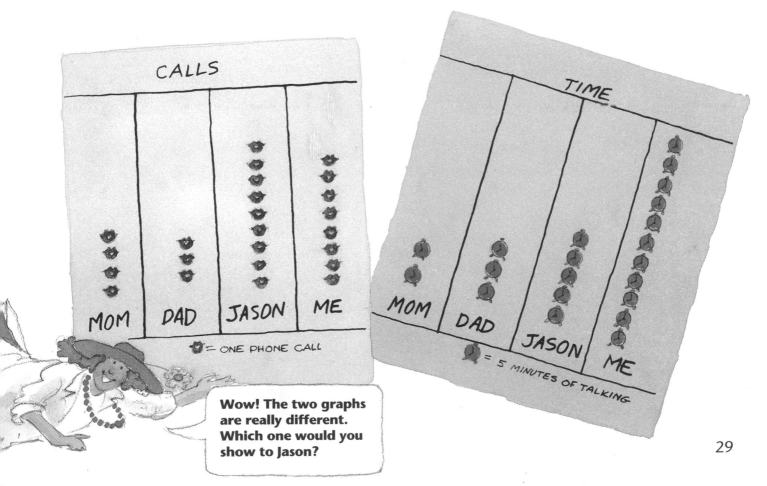

CALLS

MOM | DAD | JASON | ME

= ONE PHONE CALL

TIME

MOM | DAD | JASON | ME

= 5 MINUTES OF TALKING

Wow! The two graphs are really different. Which one would you show to Jason?

TV time

You plunk yourself down on the couch. Nora is waving her hand in front of the TV and staring.

"So, what's on?" you ask.

"The television," she replies.

"I can see that. What program?"

"Who knows?" she says, waving her hand. "This is more interesting."

The wave

What does Nora see when she waves her hand in front of the TV? Turn on the TV, hold your palm close to the screen and wave your hand back and forth. How many fingers do you see?

TV can do some weird things to you, but it can't make you grow extra fingers. So what's happening?

A television flashes thousands of dots of light about 60 times a second. Your eye doesn't see the individual flashes — it merges them into the picture on the screen. (For more about how TV works, see page 31.)

If you waved your hand back and forth as fast as the TV flashes, your hand would appear to be frozen in one position. But you  wave your hand more slowly, so you see it in several positions at once. That makes it look as if you have sprouted new fingers.

Truly exciting TV

• Turn on an electric hand mixer and hold it in front of the TV screen. Watch the beaters, not the TV. What happens as you speed up or slow down the mixer? (Ever watch old westerns? The same thing happens with the turning wheels of the stagecoaches.)

• Turn off the lights and stare at the TV. Quickly move your eyes first to the left then to the right of the screen. See anything? The image on the screen "sticks" in your vision and appears on the wall to the right of the screen.

• Tie a bolt to the end of a piece of string about 60 cm (2 feet) long. Hold the free end of the string and swing the bolt like a pendulum in front of the TV. What happens?

How a TV works

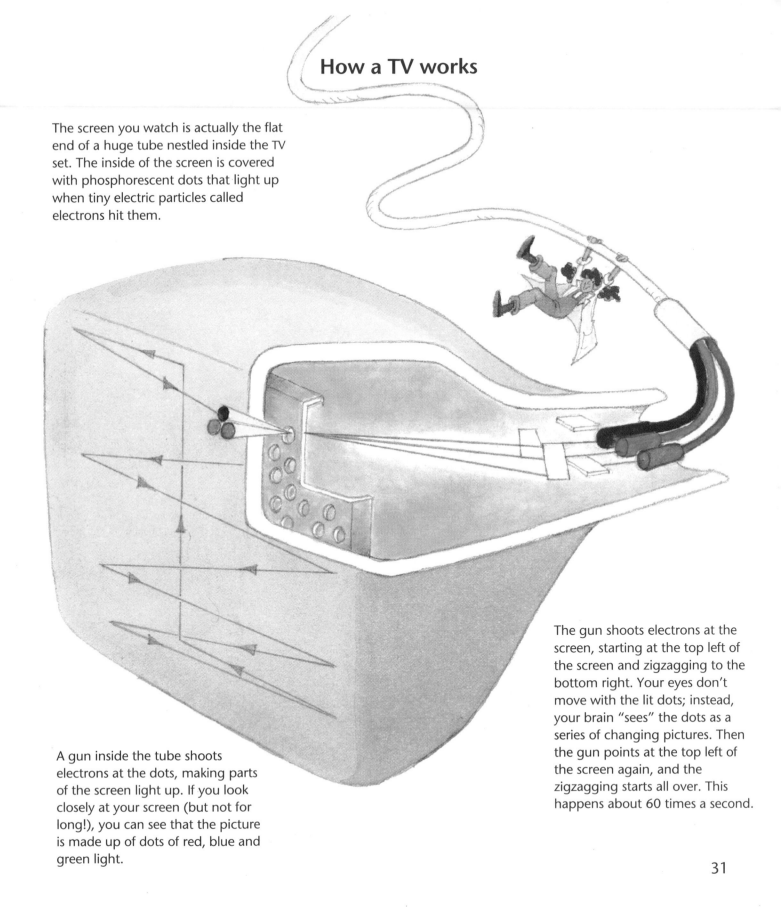

The screen you watch is actually the flat end of a huge tube nestled inside the TV set. The inside of the screen is covered with phosphorescent dots that light up when tiny electric particles called electrons hit them.

A gun inside the tube shoots electrons at the dots, making parts of the screen light up. If you look closely at your screen (but not for long!), you can see that the picture is made up of dots of red, blue and green light.

The gun shoots electrons at the screen, starting at the top left of the screen and zigzagging to the bottom right. Your eyes don't move with the lit dots; instead, your brain "sees" the dots as a series of changing pictures. Then the gun points at the top left of the screen again, and the zigzagging starts all over. This happens about 60 times a second.

31

Beddie-byes

You have begged and pleaded to watch just one more TV show, but the answer (as usual) is no. Muttering that life just isn't fair, you drag your feet towards the bathroom. Boring!

Rub a dub dub

"How can you think taking a bath is dull?" asks Nora. She is cruising around the tub in Jason's toy boat, The Moby Duck. "Take that bar of soap, for example."

You try to, but it slips out of your fingers.

"Soap doesn't actually get you clean," Nora continues, narrowly missing a rubber whale.

"Then why do we use it?"

With a flourish of her magnifying glass, Nora gives you a close-up of your (yuck, dirty!) skin.

"See the dirt? It's stuck in the oil on your skin. Now rub the soap across your skin and watch what happens. The soap lets water and the oil mix, so the water can carry off the dirt.

"It's actually the water that gets you clean, not the soap. Unfortunately, water also carries away some of the oil in your skin, which is why you're going to wrinkle like a prune if you don't get out of that bath soon."

Brush ...

"How would you like to brush your teeth with chalk, paint, detergent and seaweed?" Nora asks.

"Thanks. I'd rather use toothpaste."

"That is toothpaste. The chalk rips the layer of grunge off your teeth, the paint whitens them, the detergent makes the foam, and the seaweed sticks everything together."

"Disgusting."

"Then you probably wouldn't have liked the toothpaste the Romans used about two thousand years ago. It was made from human urine."

32

... and flush

"Speaking of urine," Nora goes on.

"Please, let's not."

"Okay, let's talk toilets."

You groan.

"Ever wonder what happens when you flush?"

Your sewage joins other waste water leaving your house. It heads out toward the street through a narrow pipe.

The narrow pipe joins a larger street pipe, which leads to a huge trunk sewer big enough for a person to walk through. Sewage and waste water may travel several kilometers (miles) through this network of pipes.

In most cities, waste water and sewage are treated in a sewage-treatment plant. Filters remove solids. Bacteria and chemicals may be used to clean up the liquids.

The solids make excellent fertilizer. The liquids are pumped into a nearby lake, river or ocean. From the time you flush, this whole journey can take up to three hours.

Zzzzzz-time

Getting ready for bed was a lot more fun than usual. In fact, life has been a lot more interesting since Nora appeared, but you'd never tell her that, of course.

You crawl under the covers and look out at the night sky framed in your window.

"You're looking back in time," Nora whispers. "Light from the stars travels at 300 000 km (186 000 miles) per second. So the light that's reaching your eyes now might have left faraway stars hundreds or even thousands of years ago. The starlight you see has come from the past."

"Mind-boggling," you murmur.

"Want to see the time you were born? Look for the star Sirius. It's about nine light-years away. That means starlight from Sirius is nine years old."

Your eyes follow her pointing finger. Then they close.

You can find Sirius with the help of a guide to the stars from your library.

CHAPTER 2
BE A SCIENTIST

Nora's clothes are usually a bit odd, but this time she has really lost it.

"You look ... " you splutter, but you just can't finish the sentence.

"Thanks," says Nora. "I'm trying on a few sciences to see how they fit." She takes off the scuba mask. "Marine biology or medical research?" She holds up the stethoscope. "Maybe I'd discover a cure for snoring."

"Experiment on Jason," you snarl.

She tries to scale a couch cushion. "Maybe I could climb mountains and become a geologist. Or be a biologist and study what bugs bugs." She waves a net with a flourish.

By the time you've got her untangled, she looks hot and tired. "This wet suit ought to be called a hot suit," she says, taking a huge gulp of the liquid in a test tube.

"Stop! What is that?" you ask. If you drank something out of a test tube, your mother would flip out.

"A magic potion. Lets you be whatever you want. Try some." She hands you the test tube. "Come on — let's be scientists."

You look at the red stuff, then at Nora. "Does it do movie stars?" you ask hopefully.

"Drink it!" she says, scowling.

You take a sip and swallow. "Cherry fizz! Nora, are you sure this is a magic potion?"

But Nora is disappearing through the corner of the page.

Be an archaeologist

You are making a sandwich when you see the tracks. "Nora!" you yell. "You walked in the butter!"

"How do you know it was me?" she asks innocently.

"You're the only thing small enough to leave these footprints."

"Could have been a mouse."

"Don't be silly. Mouse prints look like this 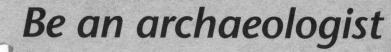, not like this ⚫︎."

"Congratulations — you've just made a deduction worthy of an archaeologist. They can figure out amazing things from evidence such as teeth or bones. Or even footprints ... "

Step back in time

The footprint on the right was found in the desert of East Africa in 1978 by a team of scientists led by archaeologist Mary Leakey. The Leakey team had been looking for animal tracks when it came across the footprint, preserved in rock that was about 3.5 million years old. The footprint was made all that time ago by one of our earliest human ancestors. The team dug carefully for almost a year and unearthed more footprints. In all, they found 24 m (80 feet) of tracks, made by two people.

What can scientists learn from a footprint? Can they figure out how tall the person was who made the footprint? Can you figure out how tall people are just by measuring their feet? Turn the page and try it.

How did the footprints get preserved in rock?

1. A volcano erupts and covers the ground with ash.

2. Later, rain falls, soaking the ash and making mud. Someone walks in the mud and leaves footprints. The sun hardens the mud.

3. Dirt and sand bury the footprints.

4. Wind or water wears away the dirt and sand. The footprints can be seen again — millions of years later.

37

FANCY FOOTWORK

You can figure out someone's height just by knowing the length of his or her foot. But like all great tricks, this takes preparation.

You'll need:

10 people to measure (Use people who have stopped growing, not young children.)
a measuring tape
a pencil and paper
a calculator

1. Measure the first person's left foot. Then measure her height. Use all centimeters or all inches.

2. Measure the other people the same way. Keep a record of everyone's foot length and height in centimeters or inches.

NAME	FOOT LENGTH	HEIGHT	PERCENT
Jasmine	24 cm	168 cm	14
Eddie	11 in.	69 in.	16
Andrew			
Sara			
Juan			

3. Now it's time to figure out if foot size and height are related. Start with Jasmine. To figure out what percentage her foot length is of her height, divide 24 by 168 and multiply by 100. The answer is 14. So Jasmine's foot length is 14 percent of her height. Now try Eddie. Divide 11 by 69 and multiply by 100. The answer is 16. Do the same calculation for all the people on your list.

4. What's the average percentage? To find out, add all the percentages and divide by the number of people. The average will be close to 15 percent.

5. You can use this average to estimate a person's height. Measure a friend's foot length. Let's say it is 9 in. So 9 in. is about 15 percent of her height. That means her total height will be about $(9 \div 15 \times 100) = 60$ in.

Measure the footprint on pages 36–37. Can you figure out the height of the person who made it? Answer on page 78.

Meet two time travelers

Archaeologists like Mary Leakey are time travelers. They use footprints and bones and objects that people have made to learn what life was like thousands of years back in time.

Mary Leakey's interest in archaeology began when she was about your age. She accompanied her artist-father to archaeological sites, where archaeologists dug for evidence of ancient people. The idea of getting a glimpse into times long past captured and held her imagination.

Sifting through dirt in the hopes of finding bits and pieces from the lives of long-dead humans is hard work. Then there are the happy accidents, such as the footprint in the rock. "In archaeology," said Mary Leakey, "you almost never find what you set out to find."

Paleontologists are also time travelers. They hunt for evidence of prehistoric animals, such as mammoths, saber-toothed tigers and even dinosaurs. The evidence? Fossils of teeth and bones and impressions of skin and footprints.

Finding the clues is half the fun. In 1812, 12-year-old Mary Anning found fossilized bones in the cliffs near her home of Lyme Regis, England. The bones were the first ever found of an ichthyosaur, a sea-dwelling animal that lived at the time of the dinosaurs. Mary collected hundreds of fossils, including ones of a previously unknown sea-dwelling animal, the plesiosaur. Thanks to Mary Anning's fossils, we know a lot about the lives of ancient animals.

ICHTHYOSAUR

PLESIOSAUR

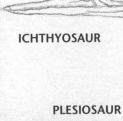

Be a geologist

"Nice lump of coal you're wearing," says Nora.

"Coal? This is 100 percent artificial silk," you say huffily. "I ought to know. I spent my birthday money on it."

"Yup, and artificial silk comes from coal. So does the dye that colored the silk yellow. Your clothes, your home, even your food are full of coal and other rocks. During your life, you'll use more than 900 000 kg (2 million pounds) of minerals — the stuff that rocks are made of."

"Wait a minute. Did you say I eat rocks?"

"Your lunch is loaded with them," says Nora.

This juice was filtered through ground-up rock.

Powdered gypsum rock is added to bread and cake icing.

Fertilizers helped grow the tomato and lettuce. Some natural fertilizers are ground-up rock.

Rock talk

The look, color and shape of rocks tell you a lot about how they were formed.

Sparkles tell you that a rock contains crystals. These are cousins of salt and sugar crystals.

Flat layered rocks began when sand and clay settled at the bottom of the sea. As more and more piled up, the stuff on the bottom had all the water squeezed out of it and hardened into rock.

40

KEEP ON ROCKING

Sometimes geologists can't tell what a rock is made of just by looking at it. This simple test tells whether a rock contains calcite.

You'll need:

*rocks — different shapes
    and colors
a nail
a lemon, cut in half*

1. Scratch each rock with the nail.
2. Squeeze some lemon juice on each scratch. If the rock fizzes, it contains calcite.

Calcite is an alkali (like baking soda). When it combines with an acid (lemon juice), it produces a gas called carbon dioxide, which bubbles up. Why do geologists want to find calcite? Because where there's calcite, there may be oil, or even gold, nearby.

Notice the stripe? This rock is actually two kinds of rock. The stripe was once hot liquid rock — like the lava that spews out of a volcano. The liquid squeezed into a crack in the other rock. Then it cooled.

No sharp edges here. Like most beach pebbles, this one has been worn smooth, probably by water tumbling the rock around.

Meet a rock star

Geologist Cathie Hickson is climbing a volcano. Every few minutes she stops and chips off a small chunk of rock. The rocks hold clues to the volcano's age. Who cares how old a volcano is? Cathie does. Part of her job is to explore young volcanoes to find out how often they have erupted and if they might erupt in the future. Cathie's research is part of a volcano-alert system to forewarn people of possible danger.

Geologists study all aspects of the Earth's rocks and minerals. A geologist probably found the oil or gas that heats your home, the metals in the jewelry you wear and, yes, even the rocks in your food.

Be a physicist

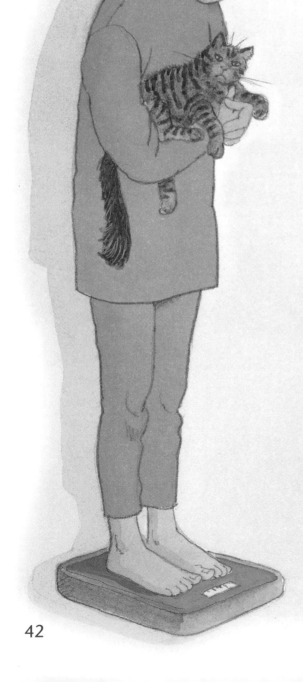

How did Spike get so fat? Was it the Tabby Treats? Too much Feline Food for dinner? Or your disappearing bedtime snacks?

"If Spike lived on the moon, she'd only weigh one-sixth of her Earth weight," Nora says, peeking over your shoulder.

"How come?"

"Bathroom scales don't measure weight," Nora explains. "They measure the Earth's gravitational pull. The moon is smaller than the Earth, so its gravitational pull is weaker. If you put Spike on a moon scale, she'd seem to weigh less. Presto — the instant moon diet."

"What about an instant Earth diet?" you ask.

"Well, you could take Spike in an elevator up a very tall high-rise."

"How would that help?"

"You know the feeling you get when a fast-rising elevator slows?"

"Like your stomach keeps on going?"

"Right. For a second or two, the pull of gravity is reduced and you experience near-weightlessness. If Spike were on the scale in an elevator as it slowed down, she'd seem to lose weight."

"All right!"

"But when the elevator stopped — instant weight gain."

Spike growls to get down. You put her on the floor, and she heads right for her food dish.

Great gravity tricks

Gravity is one of the forces that control how the physical world works. It keeps trying to pull things toward the center of the Earth. Without realizing it, you've learned to outwit gravity. Otherwise, you'd fall over every time you took a step.

How do you outsmart gravity? By carefully positioning your "center of gravity," an imaginary spot in the middle of your stomach about 8 cm (3 inches) below your belly button. It's the point around which all your weight seems to be centered. As long as you keep your center of gravity over your feet, you can stand and walk. Goof up, and you'll fall down.

You can use some gravity tricks to fool your friends.

Invisible glue

Tell your friend you are going to glue her foot to the floor with your special invisible glue. Have her stand so that one foot and the side of her head are against a wall. Pretend to squirt glue around the foot that's farther from the wall. Now tell her to raise her "glued" foot out to the side — if she can.

She would have to shift her center of gravity over her other foot, but the wall is in the way, so she can't. She's stuck.

Superfinger

Keep a friend in her place with just one finger! Have your friend sit in a chair with her head tilted back as shown. Put one finger on her forehead and press lightly. Now challenge her to get up.

In order to stand, she would have to bend forward and shift her center of gravity over her feet. But you're stopping her from doing this, with one finger.

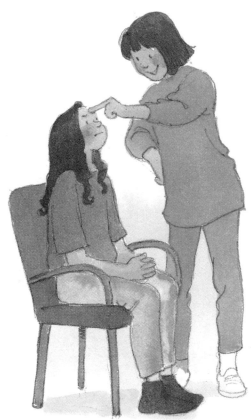

More invisible glue

Get a friend to rest her head against the wall while her feet are at least 45 cm (18 inches) away from the wall. Pretend to glue her head to the wall. Challenge her to move her head away from the wall while keeping her feet flat on the floor. Oh ... and no hands allowed.

No way. Her center of gravity is somewhere between her feet and the wall. Gravity wants to pull her center of gravity down toward the Earth. The only thing stopping her from toppling over is the wall.

Meet a spaced-out scientist

Sally Ride pushes off gently from the wall. Like a ballet dancer in slow motion, she floats across the cabin. She is weightless in the cabin of the space shuttle — there is no gravity there.

Sally Ride is a physicist, a scientist who studies the laws that govern the world around us. When a physicist sees something, she asks, "How does this work?" In the weightless environment of the space shuttle, Sally Ride asks, "How do things work without gravity pulling them down?"

One thing she and other astronauts have discovered is that they become slightly taller in space. That's because, inside space vehicles, there's no gravity to pull them down. When they return to Earth, gravity is at work again, and the astronauts "shrink" back down to their usual heights.

Be a zoologist

"Help! Help!"

Aha! Fido the cat has Nora cornered under the bed. For a second, you consider ignoring them both, but then you give in. You scoop Fido up and lock him in the basement. He is Not Happy.

"What an interesting science experiment," says Nora, trying to look dignified as she crawls out from among the dust bunnies.

"That was science?"

"Sure. Based on Fido's attempts to grab me, I determined that he's probably right-handed."

Just then, Spike gives Nora a hungry look. "I wonder if all cats are right-handed?" she asks, as she dives back under the bed.

45

IS YOUR PET A SOUTHPAW?

Are animals righties and lefties like humans? Here's your chance to be a zoologist and do some scientific research.

You'll need:

cats or dogs (use all cats or
*   all dogs, not a mix)*
a pet treat — a dog biscuit
*   or a bit of tuna (for the cats)*
a jar
adhesive tape
a pencil and paper

1. Before a pet's mealtime, put a treat in the bottom of the jar. Lay the jar on its side and tape it to the floor so it can't roll around.

2. Write down which paw the pet uses to try to get the treat.

3. Test the same pet several times. Record the results every time.

4. Test other pets — about ten in all. Make a chart to keep track of your results.

PET'S NAME	TEST 1	TEST 2	TEST 3
FIDO	R	R	L
SPIKE	L	R	L
GYPSY	R	R	R
BUFF	R	L	R
KITCAT	L	L	R
HAMISH	R	L	R
MINTY POO	R	R	L
WOODY	L	L	R
JASPER	L	R	R

What can you conclude from your results? Survey an equal number of humans. (You don't need treats; just ask if they're left- or right-handed.) Compare their answers with the pets' test results.

Melanie Watt watches cats — big cats. Melanie is a zoologist, a scientist who studies animals. She is learning about jaguars that live in the jungles of Belize. Finding jaguars to study isn't easy. They like to be left alone.

One night, Melanie put a pig in a cage as bait and climbed up onto a platform above the cage with her camera. She knew a jaguar was near when she heard the pig squeal and thrash around in the cage. No one knows who was most frightened — Melanie, the pig or the jaguar, who skittered off into the bush.

Usually Melanie studies jaguar tracks and droppings. The droppings tell her what jaguars eat. Knowing that may help save the jaguars, who are in danger of becoming extinct.

TRACKING THE WILD SPIDER

Not everyone can track jaguars — or wants to! But there's lots of other wildlife in a backyard or park. Watch a spider build a web, then preserve the web so you can look at it more closely.

You'll need:

clear plastic lacquer. (It's available at craft or hardware stores, and you'll use it again to preserve snowflakes. See page 52.)
a piece of black paper
scissors
clear plastic wrap

Collect several different webs. Find out who spun them by consulting a field guide to spiders.

1. Spray a spider web several times with lacquer. Let it dry between sprayings. It should be hard when you're done.

2. Hold the black paper under the web while you carefully cut the corner support strands.

3. Spray the web with lacquer again. When it's dry, cover it with plastic wrap to keep it from being damaged.

Be a botanist

Nora is admiring herself in the mirror.

"New necklace?" you ask.

"Made it myself," says Nora proudly. "Out of beans."

"Beans? Amazing! Show me how."

BEAN NECKLACE

You'll need:

1 or more colors of food coloring
a small bowl and spoon for each color
water
dried beans (enough for a necklace)
a strainer
paper towels
a needle and thread

1. Pour a few drops of food coloring into a bowl. If you're using several colors, put each color in a separate bowl.

2. Add about 50 mL (¹/4 cup) of water to each bowl and stir. For darker colors, add more food coloring.

3. Add your beans. The colored water should cover them. If you need to, add more water. Soak the beans for about three hours.

4. Pour the bowlful of water and beans into a strainer held over a sink. Rinse the beans and spread them out on several layers of paper towel. Repeat for each color.

5. Let the beans dry for two hours, then string them into a necklace using the needle and thread.

A bean absorbs water so that the tiny new plant inside can start to grow. Want to see a bean sprout? Try "Trick a Bean" on the next page.

48

TRICK A BEAN

Why don't plants grow upside down, with their stems underground and their roots waving in the breeze? Can you trick a plant into growing the wrong way up? Be a botanist — experiment on a bean.

You'll need:

an empty, wide-mouthed jar with a lid
paper towels
water
a pencil
5 dried bean seeds soaked overnight (Mung and pea beans work well; soy beans don't.)

1. Fold a paper towel in half. Roll it up gently and push it through the mouth into the jar. Help the paper towel unroll so it stands against the sides of the jar, as a lining.

2. Stuff crumpled-up paper towels inside the jar, to hold the lining snugly against the glass. Gently pour in about 50 mL (¼ cup) of water. Put the lid on the jar and roll it so the water soaks all the paper towels and the lining. Pour out any extra water or add more, if necessary, to dampen all the paper towels.

3. Using your pencil, poke the soaked bean seeds between the glass and the lining. Put the lid on and place the jar in a sunny spot.

4. When the beans have sprouted and you can see about 2.5 cm (1 inch) of root, turn the jar upside down. Wait a few days. What happens to the roots and stems?

How do beans know which way is up? Botanists have discovered that plants are affected by gravity. Their roots automatically grow toward the pull of gravity and their stems away from it.

Be a chemist

"Stand back!" Nora opens the oven door. The kitchen fills with delicious smells. "Wow — chocolate cake!"

"It's not cake — it's a chemistry experiment," Nora says with a sniff. She slides a crumb under her magnifying glass. "Take a look."

"Holes," you say. "Thousands of them. With a bit of cake in between."

"Right — it's those holes that make cakes light and fluffy." Nora bounces up and down on the cake. "Where'd the holes come from?"

"Ah," says Nora, doing a double back flip. "That's where the chemistry comes in."

Holey chemistry

"You need a chemical reaction to get the holes," says Nora. "Watch." She mixes some vinegar into some baking soda in a glass and, like magic, there are bubbles everywhere, including all over Nora.

"The vinegar, which is an acid, reacts with the baking soda, which is an alkali, to make bubbles of carbon dioxide gas."

"So, let me guess," you say, as you burst a passing bubble. "The same reaction happens in the cake, and the bubbles of carbon dioxide gas leave the holes."

Only one way to find out.

NORA'S CHEMISTRY CAKE

Try some kitchen chemistry and bake a cake at the same time.

Ingredients:

250 mL (1 cup) cake flour
50 mL (1/4 cup) corn or
  canola oil
175 mL (3/4 cup) sugar
1 egg
15 mL (1 tablespoon) cocoa
2 mL (1/2 teaspoon) salt
2 mL (1/2 teaspoon) vanilla
125 mL (1/2 cup) buttermilk
2 mL (1/2 teaspoon) baking soda
7 mL (1 1/2 teaspoon) vinegar

1. Preheat the oven to 180°C (350°F). Grease a 2-L (8-inch) square cake pan with a bit of butter or margarine and sprinkle it with flour.

2. Sift the cake flour into a small bowl. You should have 300 mL (1 1/4 cups) of sifted flour. If necessary, add more until you have that much.

3. Put the shortening into a large bowl and beat it with a wooden spoon. Gradually stir in the sugar. Add the egg and beat this shortening mixture till it's light and fluffy. Then stir in the cocoa and salt.

4. In a small bowl, stir the vanilla into the buttermilk.

5. In a glass, mix the baking soda and vinegar. See the carbon dioxide bubbles? Quickly stir, then pour this mixture into the buttermilk.

6. Pour some of the flour into the shortening in the large bowl. Stir. Add some of the buttermilk mixture. Stir. Continue adding flour and buttermilk, one after the other, until everything is used up. End with the flour. Stir just until everything is mixed.

7. Pour the batter into the cake pan and bake for 35 to 40 minutes. Cool and frost.

Carbon dioxide bubbles, made by combining baking soda and vinegar and by heating the batter, puffed up your cake. Carbon dioxide gas also makes bubbles in soft drinks. What would happen if you put a soft drink in the batter instead of baking soda and vinegar? Try it and see.

Use 125 mL (1/2 cup) of lemon-lime soft drink and leave out the baking soda and vinegar. Leave out the buttermilk too, so your batter isn't too wet.

The bubbles in soft drinks don't last long, so work fast!

Be a meteorologist

"Wow! What a mess."

There are bits of white paper all over the room. It looks like an indoor blizzard. A mound moves and out crawls Nora, looking very discouraged. "No matter how I cut 'em, all my snowflakes look the same."

"Cool."

"Maybe, but not scientific. Snowflakes come in lots of different shapes."

"You could use some inspiration, Nora." You pull on a jacket and hat. "Come on — let's go catch a few snowflakes."

"Won't they melt?"

"Not if you do this."

A COOL EXPERIMENT

You'll need:

a clean piece of glass at least as big as
    a soda cracker
clear plastic lacquer (available at craft and
    hardware stores)
tweezers
a magnifying glass

1. Put the glass and the lacquer into the freezer. Let them cool completely, overnight if possible.

2. Take the piece of glass out of the freezer with the tweezers. Quickly spray a thin layer of lacquer on the glass. Tilt the glass so the extra lacquer can run off. (Always handle the glass with tweezers so it doesn't get warm.)

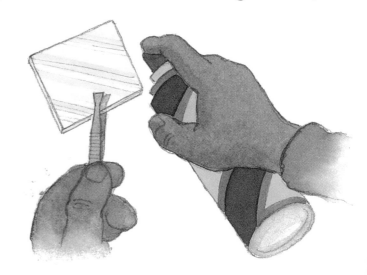

3. Put the glass outside where snowflakes can fall on it.

4. When a few snowflakes have landed on the glass, use the tweezers to carry the glass somewhere outside where no more snowflakes can fall on it.

5. After an hour, take the glass inside. (There's no need to use the tweezers this time.) You'll be able to see the impressions of the snowflakes preserved in the lacquer.

Look closely at the snowflake shapes. Are they all the same? Catch snowflakes several weeks apart. Do all snowflakes look alike? Be a meteorologist and see if different kinds of snowfalls — heavy and wet or light and dry — produce different shapes and sizes of flakes. Keep track of your results.

DATE	SNOWFLAKE	WEATHER CONDITIONS
NOV. 14		SUDDEN, WET SNOWFALL

Meet a weatherwatcher

Some meteorologists (scientists who study weather) catch snowflakes, too. By studying the flakes, they can find out about the weather that made them. Instead of waiting on the ground for the snowflakes to fall, meteorologists like Nancy Knight fly up into snowstorms in a small plane and catch snowflakes up there.

After an ordinary day of catching snowflakes above Boulder, Colorado, Nancy Knight looked through her microscope and saw this:

She had found two snowflakes that appeared to be twins. Were they identical? They seemed to be, even under a microscope. But because the weather conditions that form snowflakes change rapidly, there may be tiny differences between them.

Studying the weather can be tough because clouds and storms and blizzards don't stay put for long. Still, meteorologists are determined to find out more about it. They want to be able to forecast the weather before it happens. Why? To make sure you know when to take your umbrella? Well, yes. But they also want to warn of coming storms and other dangerous weather.

Be an environmental scientist

"Leg of mite. Flake of skin. Chunk of meteor. Sahara sand."

"Magic spell?" you ask Nora, who is staring off into space, chanting.

"Nope. Just listing some of the stuff floating in the air."

You put your hand over your mouth. "Yeccch!"

"That's not the worst of it," Nora goes on. "There's also pollution hitching a ride on the solid particles."

You put your other hand over your mouth.

"There is something you can do," says Nora slyly.

POLLUTION BUSTERS

You'll need:

sticky tape
2 unlined index cards or
    pieces of stiff white paper
2 empty jars big enough to
    tape the index cards to
a blunt knife
petroleum jelly, such as Vaseline
    (available at drugstores)

a plastic bag
a vacuum cleaner

1. Tape one index card firmly around a jar.

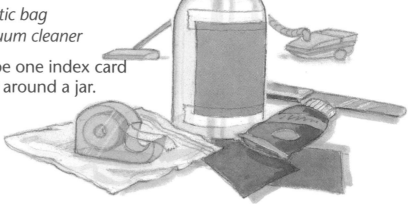

2. With the knife, spread a thin layer of petroleum jelly on the index card. This is your pollution catcher.

3. Lay the jar on its side, index card up, in your bedroom. Put it out in the open, not under the bed or other furniture.

4. Two days later, look at the index card. Has dirt from the air settled on it? Put your pollution catcher in the plastic bag.

5. Now here comes the hard part. Vacuum your room. Thoroughly. Then set up another pollution catcher in the same place you put the first one.

6. Wait two days, then compare the amount of dirt on the two index cards. Did vacuuming help?

Try putting a pollution catcher outside — near a busy street or out in the woods. Where is the dirt worst?

Was that science — or just Nora's sneaky way of getting me to vacuum my room? Think I'll get Jason to try the same experiment.

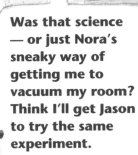

Meet an Earthwatcher

Air pollution is a big issue for environmental scientists: bad stuff in the air also ends up in our water, in the soil and, eventually, in the food we eat. Environmental scientist Beth Savan looked into the lead pollution that used to spew from car tailpipes into the air. Then she broadcast a radio series to tell people about the problem.

Environmental scientists may start out as biologists, meteorologists, botanists or other kinds of scientists. But they all end up working on the same sorts of problems. They study the effects of activities such as driving cars, running factories and building dams on the environment. Then they try to find ways to prevent the damage. To find out more about the environment, read Beth Savan's book, *Earthcycles and Ecosystems*.

Be a geneticist

Nora is staring at you so hard you feel like a germ under a microscope.

"What's wrong?" you ask nervously. (The last time someone looked at you like that you had spinach stuck to your front tooth.)

"You look like your brother, Jason," Nora says.

"Oh, please. I'd rather look like the dog."

"Sorry, but it's true. Must be your genes."

"My jeans? They were washed on Monday, which is more than you can say for Jason's jeans."

"Not jeans," says Nora. "Genes!"

Hand-me-down genes

Do people tell you that you have your mother's eyes or your father's nose? They mean that you and your parents share similar physical characteristics, or "traits." This hasn't happened by accident. Your parents passed along their genes to you. Genes help determine your eye and hair colors, your height — even the shape of your toes. Because your genes came from both your parents, you have a combination of their genetic traits. If you have brothers and sisters, they will have slightly different genetic combinations.

Sometimes one genetic trait may be linked to another. If a white cat has blue eyes, it'll probably also be deaf. Fur color, eye color and deafness — three traits — are linked in cats.

Are traits linked in humans? Find out for yourself. Do some scientific research on noses and ears.

WIGGLE AND FLARE

Can people in your family wiggle their ears? Can they also flare their nostrils? Are the two traits linked?

You'll need:

lots of ear wigglers and nostril flarers
a pencil and paper to record the results

1. Make up a chart that looks like this:

2. Start testing your subjects and write down the results. The more people you test, the more certain you can be of your results. Test at least ten people. See if there's a pattern. Can ear wigglers *always* flare their nostrils? Can some wiggle but not flare? Do the two traits seem to be linked at all?

Why can some people wiggle their ears or flare their nostrils? See page 78.

Meet a DNAgent

Imagine if you could take a firefly's ability to light up and put it into a pumpkin. You'd have a pumpkin that glows in the dark — great for Halloween!

A firefly-pumpkin is more science fiction than science. But genetic scientists *are* working on "transgenics" — plants that are improved by the addition of animal traits. Joan McPherson and her scientist associates are trying to produce plants that can withstand low temperatures. They've pinpointed the "antifreeze" genes of a fish that lives in cold arctic waters and added it to a potato plant. One day, because of their research, we may be able to grow potatoes farther north than we can today.

In the future, genetic scientists may produce some improved and unusual foods for your dinner table. If *you* could create a gene-combo food, what would it be?

And finally... be an astronomer

It is very dark in your room. You are feeling for the light switch when you see lights glowing. "Hey — the Big Dipper," you say, surprised. "Indoors!"

"Stellar observation," says a voice that can only be Nora's.

You flick on the light. "What's that weird thing?"

"This," says Nora, sliding down a shiny tube, "is a star maker. Want to make one?"

SEEING STARS

Here's how you can see the Big Dipper and other constellations indoors.

You'll need:

aluminum foil
an empty cardboard tube
   from a roll of paper towels
sticky tape
a small nail or straight pin
a flashlight (optional)

1. Tear off a piece of aluminum foil big enough to cover the cardboard tube. Wrap the foil over one end and around the length of the tube. Tape the foil in place.

2. Make the pattern of one of the constellations with a nail or pin by poking holes in the foil covering the end of the tube. (Use these constellation diagrams as a guide.)

3. Hold the flashlight up to the open end of the tube and look at the other end. If you don't have a flashlight, put the open end of the tube up to one eye and look at a bright light. You'll feel as if you're looking at a constellation up in the sky.

PISCES

AQUARIUS

CAPRICORN

SAGITTARIUS

SCORPIO

58

ARIES

TAURUS

GEMINI

CANCER

VIRGO

LIBRA

LEO

What are constellations?

Have trouble finding the North Star? It's easy to find: the end stars of the Big Dipper point to it.

Long ago, people imagined the stars linked together into patterns, called constellations, to make sense of the heavens. Eighty-eight constellations can be seen from Earth without a telescope. The 12 zodiac constellations you see here are most famous.

Meet a star

Not many people have a planet named after them, but Helen Sawyer Hogg did. Somewhere out there is Asteroid 2917, a small planet also known as "Sawyer Hogg." Dr. Hogg deserved the honor. She was an astronomer who stargazed all her life. Her special interest was the globular clusters of stars at the outermost fringes of our galaxy. By studying how they glimmered, Dr. Hogg figured out how far away they were and when they were formed.

Interested in becoming an astronomer? There are 10 000 000 000 000 000 000 000 stars like our sun in the visible universe and probably 10 000 planets that could support life. Become an astronomer and one of those heavenly bodies may be named after you.

CHAPTER 3
FLEX YOUR SCIENCE MUSCLES

You open your sock drawer and find Nora flat on her back on a bed of knee-highs. Her eyes are closed.

"Are you asleep?" you whisper.

"Are you kidding? I'm exercising."

You watch carefully but not one muscle moves. Finally you can't stand it any more. "What kind of exercise is that?"

"Brain exercise — I'm flexing my science muscles."

"Me too." You flop down on your bed and close your eyes. You've almost dozed off when something lands on your nose. You open one eye. Nora is glaring down at you.

"Up and at 'em! Time to warm up those brain cells!"

This may not be as easy as it looked.

Stuff you should know about your brain

• Most of the cells in your body are replaced several times during your lifetime. Not the nerve cells that send information to your brain. You get one set and that's it.

• Your brain is about the size and weight of a small cabbage, but it feels more like jelly that hasn't quite jelled.

• Braininess doesn't depend on brain size. If it did, an elephant would be much smarter than you. Its brain is four times the size of your brain.

Your bedroom gym

"Let's start our mental exercises here," says Nora, who has squeezed herself into a Barbie exercise outfit.

"In my bedroom?" you ask. This is a place where you rest your brain, not exercise it.

"Sure. Your bedroom is stuffed with brain-workout equipment. For starters, look at the bedspread."

You look. It's wrinkled. It's covered with cat hairs. But there's nothing special about it.

"Can you find the five-pointed star somewhere in the pattern?"

Answers on page 78.

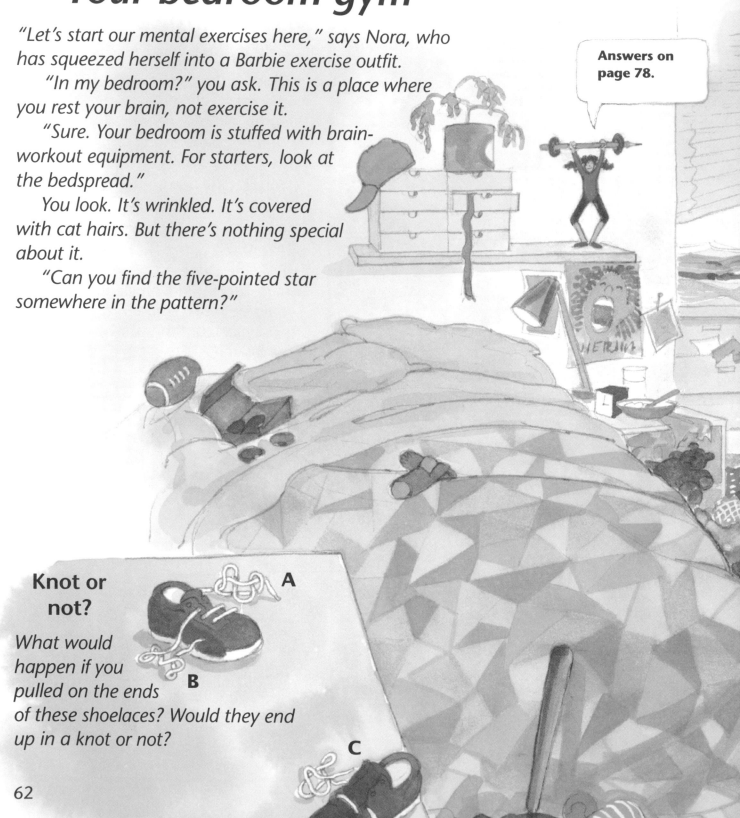

Knot or not?

What would happen if you pulled on the ends of these shoelaces? Would they end up in a knot or not?

A

B

C

The case of the dirty hands

The crumpled-up candy wrapper on your dresser is a dead giveaway. Jason the snoop has struck again. But what has he been snooping into? Your soft-drink-can piggy bank? Your jewelry box? Or—horrors—your diary?

If he tries it again, you'll be ready for him. You sharpen a pencil and brush the powder over the piggy bank, jewelry box and diary.

Later in the day, sure enough, Jason's right hand is covered in powder. Can you tell what Jason picked up by the pattern on his hand?

The jewelry-box mystery

Uh-oh! Your earrings are all mixed up. There are only two identical earrings in this bunch. Can you find the pair?

Ready for a real brain workout? Warm up by finding the twin paper dolls. The answers to all the puzzles on these two pages are on page 78.

Get the picture?

What's wrong with this picture?

Jog your eyes around this picture. Notice anything strange? Check out the shadows — they're all mixed up. Can you match the girls with their correct shadows?

Scene from above

Time to stretch your brain muscles. Here's a picnic photographed from above and, later, from the side. All the stuff has been moved around. Can you match the top view of each object with its correct side view?

64

Out of order

These six photos came in the mail with a note saying, "Put these photos in the right order, and you'll get the message." Good luck!

Hangin' or fallin'

How many of these paper clips will fall because they're not linked to any other paper clip?

65

Mirror exercises

Is your brain looking bigger? Are you looking smarter?? Are these brain exercises working??? You are checking in the mirror to see if there's any change when Nora flits by. "You can't see what you look like in a mirror."

"Why not?"

"Mirrors reverse your image left to right. Compare a picture of your face with your mirror image and you'll see the difference." She grabs a hand mirror. "If you want to see yourself as others see you, use two mirrors, like this."

"I look weird."

"Weird would be an improvement," comes a voice from Jason's room.

Fool yourself

Because mirrors reverse right and left, they can play tricks on your brain. Try some mirror exercises and see if you can get it right … and left.

• **Run a maze** Draw a simple maze on a piece of paper. Prop a mirror up against a stack of books, and position your maze so you can see it in the mirror. Put your pencil point on the start of the maze. Then, looking *only* in the mirror, draw your way through the maze. No cheating.

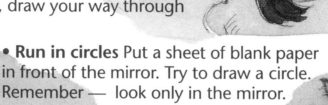

• **Run in circles** Put a sheet of blank paper in front of the mirror. Try to draw a circle. Remember — look only in the mirror.

• **Run backward** This clock is running backward because you're seeing its reflection in a mirror. What is the correct time? Answer on page 78.

Fool a friend

• Tell a friend you can turn a dime into several dollars right before her eyes. Set up two mirrors facing each other. Then put a dime between them.

The mirrors will reflect each other's image (and the dime's), so you'll see a whole lot of dimes. Adjust the mirrors and try to see more than four dollars' worth.

• What's so special about this message?

BECKIE KICKED BOB.
BOB CHOKED DICK.
DICK BOOHOOED.

Hint: it has something to do with a mirror. Give up? Turn to page 78 for the answer.

• Ask your friend to be your mirror image. Tell her to mirror everything you do. Start with an easy action, such as scratching your nose with one hand. Next, do more complicated actions, such as crossing your arms. Then move on to a series of actions. When your friend goofs up, it's your turn to be her mirror image.

67

2-D or not 2-D

Nora looks strange.

"What's wrong with you?" you ask. "Too much exercise?"

"I feel 2-D 2-day," she sighs.

"2-D? What's that?" you ask.

"Two-dimensional. Not my usual well-rounded self."

"You just look flat to me."

"Exactly. I have length and width, but no depth. Pat, the artist who draws me, usually adds shading to make me look more three-dimensional, like this."

"Of course, it's all a trick. I'm just a drawing, so I'm still only 2-D."

3-D tricks

"See this circle? It's 2-D. Add some shading and it's got bounce." She tosses you the ball.

"Perspective helps, too. You can turn a square into a box that looks three-dimensional, using perspective."

She hands you a pencil. "Draw a square, then, off to one side, a vanishing point — that's where all the lines will come together and vanish."

"Vanishing point? As in 'disappearing'? I'd like a vanishing point for Jason." You look at what you've drawn. "So where's the box?"

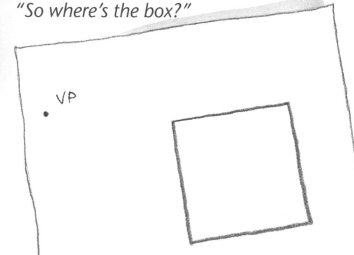

VP

"Draw lines from the corners of the square to the vanishing point. You can make a big box or a small box, depending on where you draw the top and side lines."

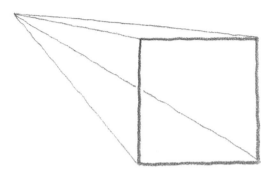

"Add some shading and you've got a box you could mail a dumbbell in."
"A dumbbell like Jason? I wish."

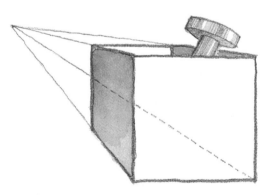

Try moving the vanishing point around and see what happens to the shape of your box.

FROM 2-D TO 3-D

You can make boxes, pyramids and other 3-D objects by taping together 2-D squares and triangles.

1. Cut out 12 squares, each 5 cm x 5 cm (2 inches x 2 inches). Cut four of the squares in half diagonally to make eight triangles.

2. Tape the squares and triangles together to make three-dimensional shapes.

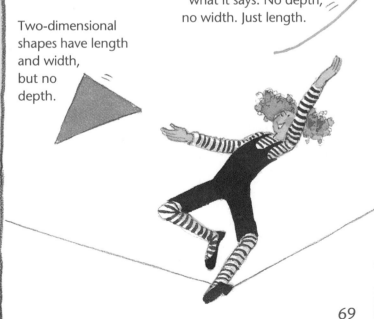

Three-dimensional objects have length, width and depth.

One dimension means what it says. No depth, no width. Just length.

Two-dimensional shapes have length and width, but no depth.

69

Feeling bagged?

"Hey, Nora! Want to go bowling?"

No answer. No Nora. Nothing but mounds of clothes and piles of junk as far as the eye can see. Your room is definitely out of control. You hear a faint "Zzzzzzzzz" and track it to a paper bag. You peer in. There she is. Asleep.

"Nora. Wake up. Let's go bowling."

"Lemerslp."

"What?"

"Let. Me. Sleep."

"Nora! I need help. I'm going bowling. Dad has loaned me his bowling ball, but I need something to carry it in."

"Invent a bag," she says, as she rolls over and curls up. "Margaret Knight did."

"Did what?"

"Invented the flat-bottomed paper bag. You probably need a round-bottomed one."

"Cool. Let's bag this ball."

"Zzzzzzzzz."

Looks as if you're on your own.

Meet an inventor

What's so special about a flat-bottomed paper bag? It sits on a table without falling over, and you can put more stuff in it than in other bags. Margaret Knight invented a machine to make flat-bottomed paper bags in 1867.

That wasn't her first invention — or her last. Her first was a device to stop the shuttle from flying off weaving looms and injuring people. She invented it when she was only 12 years old. Altogether, she invented close to 30 tools and machines.

70

IT'S IN THE BAG

Carefully cut a large paper grocery bag along the lines where it has been glued. When you flatten it out, it doesn't look much like a paper bag, does it?

A paper bag is a great carry-all. But not for a weird-shaped object like a bowling ball. Try designing a bag for a bowling ball. Or how about bagging a lamp? Or a fish?

You'll need:

a pencil and paper
several large sheets of paper bigger than
  the object you want to bag
scissors
glue or sticky tape

1. On your small piece of paper, sketch what the finished bag will look like.

2. Imagine what your bag would look like if it were flattened out. Sketch a small pattern for it. (Remember what happened when you flattened out the paper bag — it looked very different from what you expected.)

3. Draw a large version of your pattern on a big piece of paper. Cut it out and fold it into the finished shape. Glue or tape it together.

If your finished bag doesn't look as if it would hold the object it was designed for, change your pattern and try again.

A clothes encounter

Your bowling ball is in its new bag. All you need is your shark T-shirt and you're ready to go. Now where is it? You tiptoe around, quietly lifting mounds of clothes and moving piles of junk. You don't want to wake Nora. You have a strange feeling you've done this before.

As you sit down on the bed, two things happen. You spot your T-shirt and hear a squeal. This is feeling more and more familiar.

Nora crawls out from under the covers. "Can't a body get some rest?"

"Oops! Sorry to wake you, Nora." You're not really sorry at all. Nora has kept you hopping for the past few days. Maybe it's her turn for some brain work.

"Hey, Nora. Are you up for one last brain exercise?" How can she say no? "My shark T-shirt is somewhere in this room. This message will tell you where." You grab a pen and start writing — in code.

73

How to Use This Book to Do a Science Fair Project

This is Hilary Morrice, with her award-winning science fair project, "There's More to Feet than Meets the Nose." It all started when Hilary heard about "Fancy footwork" on page 38. (Hilary is a friend of the author's, so she got a sneak preview of what would be in this book.)

For her science fair project, Hilary came up with the hypothesis that there was a relationship between foot length and body height. Then she devised an experiment to test her hypothesis: she measured the feet and the height of 88 people of all ages. She kept careful records of the measurements and the ages of her subjects. Next, she analyzed the measurements (data) and prepared graphs to show the results. Because she had kept track of the ages of her test subjects, she could also tell whether the relationship between foot length and height was the same for all ages. Finally, she

74

came up with a conclusion that showed how her results proved or disproved her hypothesis.

Eighty-eight feet? What a feat! The more data you have, the more reliable your conclusion will be.

Hilary's science fair project followed a process called "the scientific method": begin with a hypothesis, test it with an experiment, analyze the results and draw a conclusion. Many of the experiments in this book can become science fair projects that test hypotheses using the scientific method. See the following page for some ideas.

The questions will help you come up with a hypothesis.

•A toast test (p. 10): Does cooking change starch into a form of sugar in other foods?

•Snap, crackle and sog (p. 11): Does one brand of paper towel soak up more liquid than another?

•Seeing the invisible (p. 14): Do different microorganisms prefer different foods?

•Amaze-ink! (p. 16): Can other substances besides ink be separated using chromatography?

•A mouth-watering experiment (p. 21): Will saliva break down all foods? How long does it take?

•Is your pet a southpaw? (p. 46): Are cats more likely to be lefties than dogs?

•Pollution busters (p. 54): Does the distance away from a busy street affect the amount of dirt collected?

•Wiggle and flare (p. 57): Are girls more able to wiggle or flare than boys?

Not all science fair projects follow the scientific method. Some show how something works:

Go to the library to find answers to these questions.

•A toast test (p. 10): How does iodine act as a starch indicator? Try the iodine test on laundry starch, sawdust and a variety of other foods and substances.

•Rain or shine? (p. 13): How does a hygrometer predict rain? How do professional meteorologists predict rain?

•A mouth-watering experiment (p. 21): How do saliva and other digestive juices break down food?

•Frisbee fun (p. 25): How do things fly?

•And flush (p. 33): How does a sewage-treatment plant work?

•How did the footprints get preserved in rock? (p. 37): How do things get preserved for millions of years?

Other science fair projects are collections of things:

•The good, the bad and the ugly (p. 15): Collect and describe a variety of microorganisms.

•Keep on rocking (p. 41): Mount a rock collection containing a wide variety of rocks. Test them for calcite.

•Tracking the wild spider (p. 47): Collect spider webs and present information on who made them.

•A cool experiment (p. 52): Assemble a snowflake collection and facts on snow.

Make sure your science fair project is fun and informative.

Choose a topic that interests you — you'll spend lots of time working on it. Use pictures, colored paper and lettering that's easy to read to make your final presentation appealing and interesting.

Note to Parents, Teachers and Group Leaders

A science book for girls? Isn't science gender-free? Yes and no. While science isn't male, most of the people who work in the sciences are. Only about one in ten science and engineering workers in the United States, Great Britain and Canada is female. Women are losing out on jobs that pay more than traditional female occupations.

For some time, researchers have been asking why so few young women choose science-related careers. Theories include the lack of female role models and mentors, girls' underdeveloped spatial visualization skills* and learning styles incompatible with the scientific method practiced by men. Whatever the reasons, one thing is clear: girls begin to "turn off" science at an early age.

The Science Book for Girls and Other Intelligent Beings was written to give 8- to 12-year-old girls a positive experience of science and science careers before they hit their teens, when educational and career decisions are made. It is hoped that the book will help guide girls along a path being cleared by such organizations as the Society for Canadian Women in Science and Technology (which was instrumental in the preparation of this book), the Women Inventors Project, the Minerva Project and hundreds of other science-for-girls courses across North America.

Parents, teachers and group leaders can positively affect girls' attitudes to science.

At home

•Explore with your daughter questions about the world. If you don't know the answers, work together with her to figure things out. Show her how to track down answers in books. There are many excellent science-activity books that give children hands-on experience of otherwise abstract science concepts.

•Bring math and science into daily life. Cook together in the kitchen — double a recipe or halve it; change one ingredient in a favorite recipe and observe the effect. Give your daughter problems to solve — a door handle or toy to fix, an old clock, radio or toaster to take apart. Provide her with pliers and other basic tools.

•On a trip, work on map skills, collect rocks, look for unusual insects or see the stars away from city lights. Take along a small science kit containing a magnet, magnifying glass, small fish net, plastic bags and small bottles.

•Try some building activities. If you're not handy with wood and tools, use rolled-up newspapers, store-bought building sets, even uncooked spaghetti joined with glue or marshmallows. Building things exercises the spatial visualization skills that may be underdeveloped in girls because of the activities they tend to favor. Visual puzzles (see Chapter 3) also build spatial visualization skills.

•Visit science museums, parks staffed by nature interpreters, planetariums and other places where science meets the public. Many industries also offer guided tours of their plants — visit an auto-assembly plant, an oil or soap factory. Ask the scientists and technologists lots of questions; encourage your daughter to do so, as well.

•If possible, enroll your daughter in after-school or summer science camps. Studies show that girls flourish — and gain self-confidence — in all-girl science groups.

•If you work in a science-related field, volunteer to give a career talk at your daughter's school. One scientist adopted a school for a year. She planned a variety of programs and got to know (and inspire) many kids.

•Introduce your daughter to books and videos about women scientists. Many of their stories are not commonly known, and girls need such role models.

In school

Many ideas suggested above can be adapted for schools and groups. Here are several tips to boost girls' enthusiasm for science in group situations:

•Monitor your responses to girls' and boys' science questions. Boys often get more feedback than girls do, even from women teachers.

•Emphasize the connection between science and the everyday world. Try to bring "girl culture" into the science curriculum. Discussing volts and amps? Use a hair dryer as your example. If you are using objects and situations that are less familiar to girls, give them time to become comfortable before proceeding.

•Foster an atmosphere that allows girls to take risks — and not to be afraid of failure. Science involves uncertainties and learning from the unexpected.

•Start an all-girl after-school or lunch-time science club. A binder of girl-tested group activities called *Imagine the Possibilities* is available from the Society for Canadian Women in Science and Technology, Room 140 - 515 West Hastings St., Vancouver, BC, V6B 5K3 Canada. A useful activity-filled book is *How to Encourage Girls in Math and Science*, by J. Skolnick, C. Langbrot and L. Day (Dale Seymour Publishers, P.O. Box 10888, Palo Alto, California, 94303-0879). Write for prices and ordering information.

Whether at home or at school, encourage girls in their science undertakings. Many females turn off science not because they are actively *dis*couraged but simply because they are not *en*couraged.

* Spatial visualization is the ability to recognize spatial relationships and to mentally manipulate objects in space. It is thought to be an important component of mathematical thinking.

Answers

Math to keep you dry, page 12:

Walking: 10 minutes x 200 drops a minute = 2000 drops

Running: 5 minutes x 150 drops a minute = 750 drops. Add to this the drops you run into: 5 minutes x 75 drops = 375 drops. Total drops: 750 + 375 = 1125 drops. So you'd stay drier running.

The great sandwich divide, page 22: Of the nine sandwiches, you give the four girls one and eat one yourself. You have (9 - 5) 4 sandwiches left. You cut these in half, so you have (4 x 2) 8 sandwich halves. You and the four girls each take a half, which leaves (8 - 5) 3 halves. You cut these halves in half again and get (3 x 2) 6 quarter-sandwiches. You and the four girls each take a quarter (6 - 5) = 1. After you hide one quarter, there is none left.

Different dogs, page 27: *Boil 'em:* The wiener rolls over about every 30 seconds. Why? As the bottom part, which is in boiling water, heats up, the air in it expands. This makes it less dense than the colder "up" side of the wiener, so it flips.

Fry 'em: The side of the wiener touching the pan heats first and expands. The other side doesn't expand. So the wiener curls.

Nuke 'em: The microwaves agitate water molecules in the wiener. Its skin isn't strong enough to withstand the bouncing water molecules, so it splits open. Punching holes in the wiener with a fork gives the water molecules an escape route.

Mushy buns: Water in the bun heats up and steams the bun, making it mushy. Leave it too long and all the water will evaporate. It will become a solid lump.

Fancy footwork, page 38: The footprint on pages 36–37 is about 21.5 cm (8.5 inches) long. So the height of the person who made the footprint would be (21.5 ÷ 15 x 100) 143 cm or (8.5 ÷ 15 x 100) 56 inches.

Wiggle and flare, page 57: Some people have tiny muscles that allow them to wiggle or flare. These muscles are probably leftovers from millions of years ago. Think of a horse. Tiny twitching muscles under its skin help the horse flick off pesky flies. Its flaring nostrils can enlarge to gather more smell information. Maybe wiggling and flaring had a use for early humans, too.

Your bedroom gym, page 62:

Knot or not?, page 62: None of the shoelaces would end up knotted.

The case of the dirty hands, page 63: The soft-drink-can piggy bank.

The jewelry-box mystery, page 63:

Get the picture?, page 64: 1 and 4 are the twin paper dolls.

What's wrong with this picture?, page 64: 1C, 2D, 3E, 4A, 5B

Scene from above, page 64: 1D, 2A, 3C, 4B, 5F, 6E

Out of order, page 65: The correct order of the photos is: 3, 5, 2, 6, 1, 4.

The secret message is: Nora was here!

Hangin' or fallin', page 65: One. The purple paper clip will fall.

Run backward, page 66: According to the clock, it's 1:25. Hold the clock up to a mirror to check it.

BECKIE KICKED BOB ..., page 67: Hold the sentence in front of a mirror upside down.

A clothes encounter, page 72: The "3" at the beginning of the message tells you to read only every third letter. Now you can solve the puzzle.